IMAGES
of America

WARREN

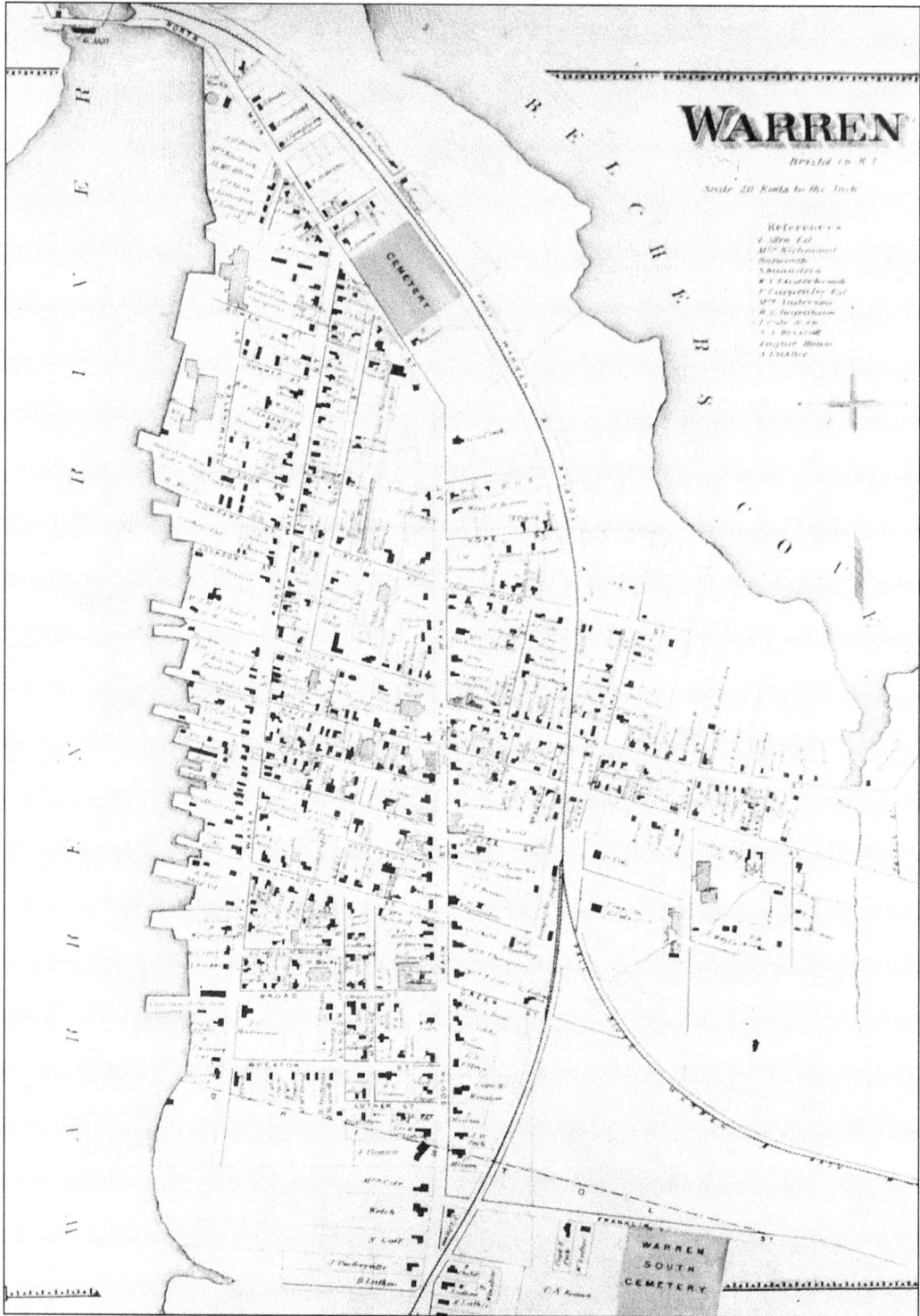

WARREN

Bristol Co. R.I.

Scale 20 Rods to the Inch

References

CEMETERY

WARREN
SOUTH
CEMETERY

FRANKLIN ST.

BROAD

LUTHER ST.

IMAGES
of America

WARREN

Ruth Marris Macaulay and John Chaney

ARCADIA
PUBLISHING

Published by Arcadia Publishing
Charleston SC, Chicago IL, Portsmouth NH, San Francisco CA

Library of Congress Catalog Card Number: 2008941578

For all general information contact Arcadia Publishing at:
Telephone 843-853-2070
Fax 843-853-0044
E-mail sales@arcadiapublishing.com
For customer service and orders:
Toll-Free 1-888-313-2665

Visit us on the Internet at www.arcadiapublishing.com

The Maxwell House, c. 1755, now the home of the Massasoit Historical Association.

Contents

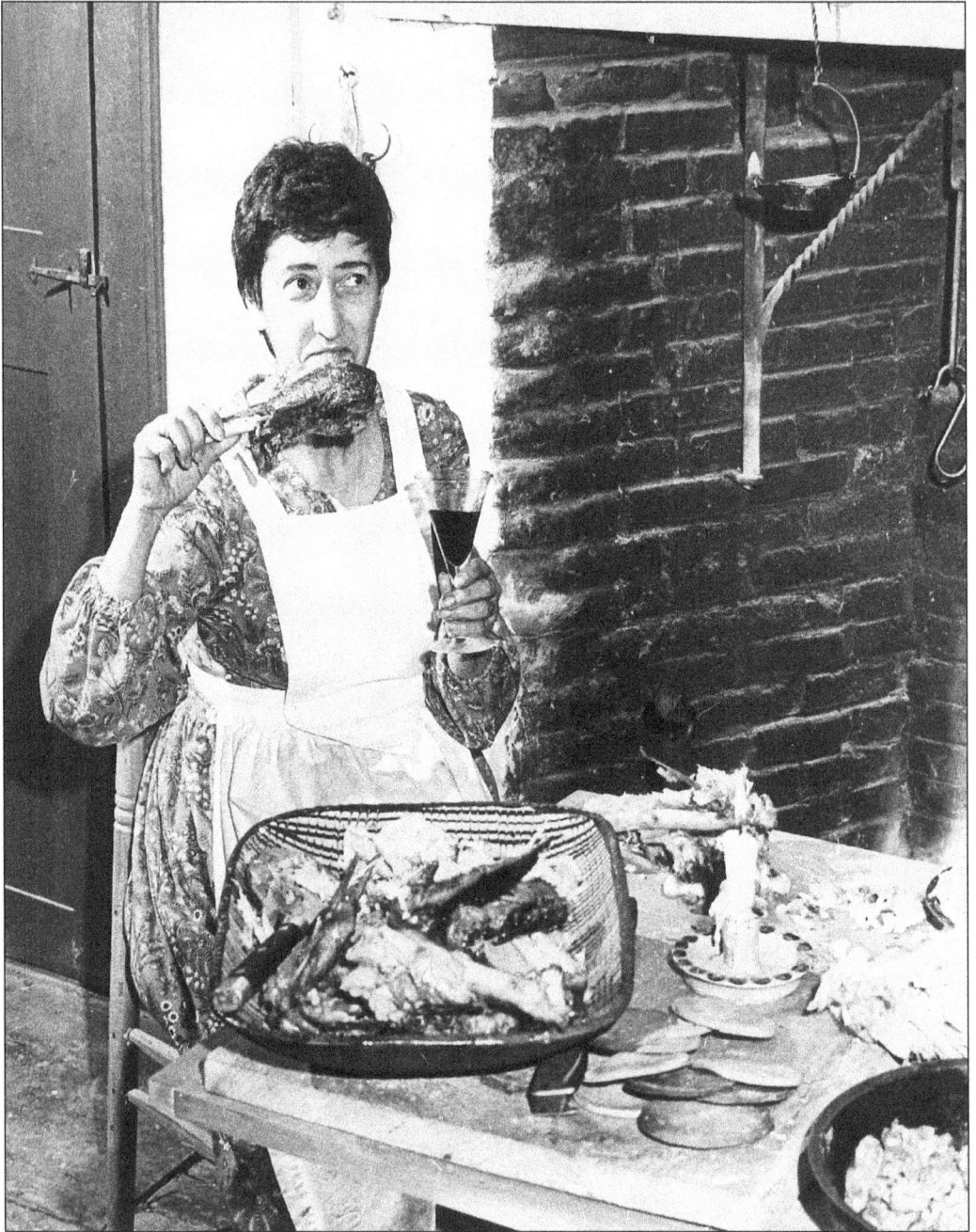

In affectionate memory of Mary Rose Niewodowski
1930–1995

Introduction

Warren grew up alongside the Warren River on the site of the Wampanoag camp site of Sowams. It was easily accessible from both sea and land, and had a freshwater spring (commemorated today as Massasoit's Spring, at the foot of Baker Street), advantages that recommended it to its first and subsequent settlers.

> "'Twas here in Sowams that with native grace
> Her good chief hailed the stranger from afar
> But ah! he saw not in the white man's face
> The red man's setting star.
>
> He little dreamed how soon the entering tide
> Would push his hapless people far aside
> And quench their wigwam fires."

So wrote George M. Coomer (1825–1901), local poet and editor of the *Warren Gazette*, referring to the Wampanoags' first encounter with white men. Decimated by a plague, probably smallpox, just before the Pilgrims arrived on Cape Cod, the Wampanoag warriors had been reduced from three thousand to three hundred when Edward Winslow and Stephen Hopkins journeyed from Plymouth in 1621 to visit their sachem Massasoit. With them they brought a laced red coat and copper chains as gifts. Two years later, when word of the sachem's illness reached Plymouth, Winslow returned with John Hampden. He was able to restore Massasoit's health, win his friendship, and, by 1632, establish an English trading post on the west bank of the Kickemuit River.

In March 1653 Massasoit sold Sowams and a plot of land for £35. In 1667 this land, which included the present towns of Warren and Barrington in Rhode Island, and Somerset, Massachusetts, was incorporated by the Court of Plymouth as the town of Swansea, Massachusetts. The central part of modern Warren and Bristol, Mount Hope Neck, was reserved for the Native Americans. A cordial relationship with the English settlers continued, and Roger Williams benefited from this friendship when he fled from Massachusetts to found Rhode Island in 1636.

After Massasoit's death in 1661 he was a succeeded by his oldest son Wamsutta (also known as Alexander). By this period the Native American population had become increasingly anxious about the encroachment on its lands by white settlers. Wamsutta's death on his way home from Plymouth in 1665, after his forcible arrest on a false rumor that he was plotting a rebellion, ended the peaceful relationship with the English. Wamsutta's brother Metacomet (known as King Philip) began a bloody war that kept New England in turmoil until 1677. On June 20, 1675, King Philip's War began with the plunder of Sowams. All the homes of English settlers were burned and the heads of eight Englishmen stuck up on poles.

The war ended in 1677, and by 1682 house and farm lots for a new settlement, known as Brook's Pasture, were surveyed and divided on the site of what was to become Warren. Further sites were surveyed in the north section of Warren in 1725. In 1747, by a royal decree, Rhode Island incorporated Barrington and small parts of Rehoboth and Swansea into the new town of Warren, named after British naval hero Admiral Sir Peter Warren, who had been victorious at the Battle of Louisbourg in June 1745. The first town meeting (a political institution still in existence today) was held on February 10, 1747. The census of 1748 shows the population of Warren to be 380 with 30 Native Americans.

Warren's deep river channel and its gently sloping shores led to the development of shipbuilding and a maritime economy. Wharves, cooperages, rope walks, and sail lofts proliferated along the waterfront before the Revolution. Coastal, slave, and West Indies trade was established as well as some whaling. The Revolutionary War and the capture of Newport threatened to ruin Warren's commercial base. On May 25, 1778, British and Hessian troops raided the town and burned a substantial number of ships and boats as well as the Baptist meeting house and parsonage. In the fall of 1778 the town was visited by the Marquis de Lafayette for several months, his main camp being near Windmill Hill. He was reputed to have enjoyed the johnny-cakes served at Cole's Tavern, an inn on the corner of Joyce and Main Streets. Burr's Tavern, another Warren hostelry that once stood on Main and King Streets, extended its hospitality to George Washington on March 13, 1781. King Street was renamed Washington Street in his honor.

After the Revolutionary War, Warren's reputation as a whaling port grew steadily, and by 1830 the port was home to twenty-six whalers. It became the seventh largest whaling port on the East Coast, far outstripping other Rhode Island seaport towns, including both Providence and Newport. Fortunes were made in whaling that are still evident in some of the architecture and architectural embellishments undertaken during this period. Warren ships also carried hopeful young men in search of adventure to the gold regions of California.

By 1847, however, Warren had followed in the wake of other Rhode Island towns and had built its first cotton mill, a stone structure on north Water Street. This was followed by two further brick mills in 1860 and 1873. All three buildings were destroyed by fire in 1895, but the town's economic focus had, by then, shifted from maritime industries to textiles. A new mill was begun in 1896, one that still stands today.

Although a substantial part of the town's economy became based on the mills, Warren always retained links with the sea. Boats are still built and repaired along the waterfront. Oyster fishing, established by the Wampanoags in Sowams, thrived in the 1880s and 1890s, and continued until the 1938 hurricane wreaked havoc with the oyster beds. Today, the shellfish-processing industry is present at Blount Seafood.

The photographs in this book allude to all the phases of Warren's past, although the majority of them were taken after 1870 and before 1970. They tell the tale of

> Warren, fair town beside the placid river
> Through which the old ships sought the treasured sea
> Green-walled with trees, the summertime forever
> Celestial brightness bring thy shores and thee.

—Hezekiah Butterworth (1809–1905), Warren poet

Ruth Marris Macaulay (Head of History Dept., Lincoln School, Providence, R.I. 02906)
John Chaney (President, Massasoit Historical Association, Warren, R.I. 02885)
May 1996

One

Through Cady's Lens

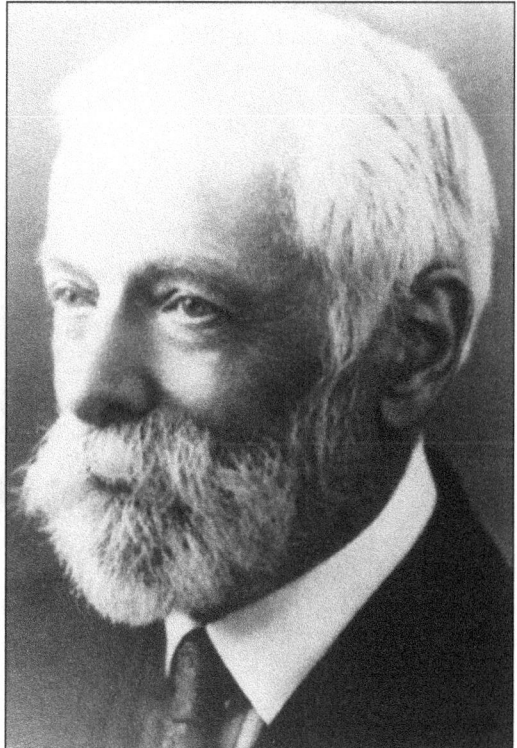

Henry Newell Cady, born in Warren in 1849. The son of Warren's first high school principal, Cady graduated from Brown University in 1869. He became a photographer as well as a photo engraver, painter, and illustrator, with a preference for marine subjects. In addition to these talents, Cady was both a writer and a composer and played the organ at a number of local churches. He set his stamp on an era of Warren's history and a number of his photographs are included in this collection. Henry Cady died in 1935.

Henry Cady in 1868.

Cady in 1902.

An illustration by Henry Cady from "The Old School Bell," a poem written by Warren poet Hezekiah Butterworth (1809–1905) for the first reunion of the Warren High School Alumni Association, September 30, 1887.

THE OLD SCHOOL BELL.

WARREN, fair town beside the placid river,
Through which the old ships sought the treasured sea,
Green walled with trees; the summer time forever
Celestial brightness
brings thy shores and thee.

The Thomas Cole House, c. 1850, on Union Street. This residence was built by Thomas Cole, whose daughter Annie lived here with her husband, Warren photographer Henry N. Cady. It was later the home of Lydia E. Rogers, a well-loved Warren schoolteacher.

Union Street, looking south. "Mr. Collamore is getting in his coal," Henry N. Cady wrote of this picture, taken from his rooftop on Monday, July 17, 1882, at 9:30 am.

The Charles Wheaton Jr. House, c. 1830, on Liberty Street. This structure was built by the son of the proprietor of one of Warren's main rope walks, John R. Wheaton, who lived across the street. Henry Cady took the photograph from an upstairs window.

Is it Monday . . . washday? Henry Cady took this picture looking north to Miller Street from the steeple of the Methodist church.

On the waterfront. The Warren River, taken from the steeple of the Methodist church by Henry N. Cady.

Members of the Cady family in a horse-drawn vehicle.

A clambake at Juniper Farm, August 2, 1891. The Cady family entertained many friends and townspeople at this gathering by the Kickemuit River.

Summer at Juniper Farm, 1891. The Cadys spent their summers in this pleasant riverside dwelling.

A quiet afternoon at Juniper Farm, 1891.

Two

Gone but
Not Forgotten

"The Old Ark." In 1680 a part of the Old Ark was built. Robert Joll, the original owner, gave it its name because, like Noah's Ark, it sheltered eight souls. The house, except for one foot at the northwest corner, was in Bristol before the town line was moved in 1873. A small portion of the yard also extended into Warren. The main road, now Main Street, was originally a turnpike and people passing between the towns paid their toll at Joll's Gate. The Ark was torn down in 1894 to make way for St. Mary's Institute, itself torn down in 1959. St. Mary of the Bay Church now stands at this location.

North Water Street at the junction of Main Street.

The General Nathan Miller House (see following page) on Miller Street west of Water Street.

The General Nathan Miller House, built before the Revolution and now demolished. General Miller was a hero of the Revolutionary War. Town lore has it that the family made a dramatic escape, under enemy fire, by boat to Barrington when the British raided Warren in 1778. The house was ransacked, the looters quenching their thirst with the General's cider which they compelled his slave Flora to taste first to see if it was poisoned. They departed lamenting that they had not "got hold of the fellow in the big boots." General Miller, a man of substantial proportions, was said to have boots that could hold a bushel of corn apiece and a vest that could be buttoned around four boys. Guests to the home included George Washington, the Marquis de Lafayette, and the Comte de Rochambeau.

The eighteenth-century Baker House, at the northwest corner of Water and Baker Streets. Legend has it that when Warren was pillaged by the British in 1778, the Baker House was visited by a party of Hessians who had just ransacked the home of General Nathan Miller. Various articles belonging to the Bakers caught their fancy. Mrs Baker wore around her neck a kerchief of checked homespun. This, despite her remonstrances, was appropriated by a soldier, a burly Hessian who signified by gesture he wanted something from the top shelf of a closet. Mrs. Baker was forced to mount a chair and submit dish after dish for his inspection. As none were what he desired, she felt he was intentionally annoying her. Soon an officer passed through the room and, observing what the fellow was about, addressed him in German, at the same time striking him across the face with a whip which Mrs Baker recognized as being the property of General Miller. The man sulked away and the gallant officer assisted the relieved lady to the floor. The house burned down in 1906.

20

The doorways of 395 Water Street (left) and 25 Washington Street (right), both now demolished. As Warren's maritime economy brought wealth to the town, the architecture became increasingly elaborate and "high style."

The home of Captain Alfred Barton. This building, built in 1863 at the northwest corner of Main and Miller Streets, was demolished to make room for a Dunkin' Donuts.

Joseph Hutcheson's House, Warren, R. I.

The residence, now no longer standing, of the Reverend Joseph Hutcheson, minister of St. Mark's Episcopal Church.

The garden of the Hutcheson House.

Three

With Us Still

The Bosworth Mansion, built around 1840 on Federal Street. Later, a separate nearby building housed Maxfield's Ice Cream Parlor, a fondly remembered establishment.

Main Street looking north from Market Street in 1890. On the right is the early nineteenth-century Polly Sanders House.

The Polly Sanders House, *c.* 1802, later owned by Dr. M. Merchant.

The Dow-Starr House on Main Street, c. 1860. This building became the convent for St. Jean Baptiste Catholic Church, and was later converted into an apartment building.

The Nathaniel Drown House on the southwest corner of Main and Liberty Streets.

"The Junction" of Main and Water Streets looking south, at the turn of the century. The building in the center is no longer standing.

The west side of Water Street looking south from "The Junction," c. 1890.

Water Street looking north from Broad Street.

Mantels from the Miller-Abbott House, Miller Street.

The corner of Miller and Union Streets. The Rudolphus B. Johnson House, c. 1800, shows Federal and Greek Revival features.

The Stockford House, early nineteenth century. Built on Broad Street, this residence has its entrance to one side.

Looking down Baker Street from
Main Street in 1890.

An interior view of the Bliss-Ruisden
House, c. 1825, on Main Street.

The Thompson House, a colonial house with Victorian alterations, on the east side of Main Street, south of the library.

The Bliss-Ruisden House, c. 1825, before the colonial revival fence from Barrington was added. It was known locally as Dr. Forget's House.

The Mrs. Thomas Carr House on Main Street, which later became known as the Wilmoth House. It was ultimately converted into the Columbus Credit Union.

The corner of South Main and Bridge Streets.

A postcard of the residential section of south Main Street.

Four

Business Ventures

Warren wharves and shipyards, from the 1877 bird's-eye view. From the early eighteenth century until around 1850, the town's economy, aside from farming, was predominantly maritime. Ships from Warren were involved in trade with the West and later the East Indies. They also traded up and down the colonial coast and were partially involved in the notorious slave trade known as the " triangle trade." Whaling began in a small way in the late eighteenth century, but boomed between about 1830 and 1850.

"The Stone Pier" and "The Beacon" on the Warren River, taken in 1882. "The Pier" was built around 1830 to mark the position of a ledge that had proved a considerable menace to shipping in the river. A directional arrow atop the beacon pointed to the safe channel to the east. The pier also had a small shed used by oystermen. In 1848 it was used as a quarantine station when the *Hoogly*, a whaling ship, returned from a voyage with four cases of smallpox. By this time the shed had been enclosed and made comfortable. One of the crew died from the disease and was buried on the Barrington shore. Local historian George H. Commer wrote "Poor Old Pier! Gay parties have landed upon it . . . sailboats have bumped right into it in the dark . . . ice has crashed against it, and all the fury of the Narragansett has assailed it in storms." With the passing of the years both pier and shed have disintegrated.

The bark *Coloma*, built at the foot of Washington Street in 1869 by James Jerome Cady. The *Coloma* carried a crew of ten. Her home port was Providence, but was later taken to the Pacific coast. On December 7, 1906, she was abandoned at sea off Cape Beale, British Columbia, with no loss of life.

The Massasoit Oyster Company on Water Street.

Oystermen at the Massasoit Oyster Company.

Warren fishermen at lunch.

An oyster boat near Barton's Wharf.

Dredging for oysters.

Aboard an oyster boat.

The George T. Greene Oyster Company. Started by George T. Greene Jr. in 1896, the company was situated near the foot of Beach Street. It was severely damaged in the 1938 hurricane.

A building built on a wharf at the foot of Barton's Wharf, between Miller and Baker Streets. Many wharves had buildings built on them similar to the one in this August 7, 1889 photograph.

The Warren waterfront.

The Gardner Brown Mill (left) in 1944, constructed in 1848 for the whaling industry. This mill, which has served as a sail loft and then the Narragansett Oyster Company, retains its links with Warren's maritime past by serving as the home of Blount Seafood.

Workers at Blount Seafood picking clams. Notice the Campbell's soup inspectors in the background against the right-hand wall.

Mill workers in the weaving room. In 1847 the Warren Manufacturing Company constructed its first small stone mill on north Water Street, where it expanded in 1860 and 1873. Cutler Manufacturing began in 1869 and Parker Mills in 1879. The development of the textile industry presented new employment opportunities. In 1860 the town's population was 2,636. The addition of nearly one thousand new people between 1870 and 1875 reflects these changes.

The overseer and foremen of the Warren Manufacturing Company mill.

Young women folding bolts of cloth.

A view of the weaving room.

Mill girls pose for a group photograph.

A maintenance crew in the boiler room of the mill.

A detail from the 1877 bird's-eye view of Warren highlighting the Warren Manufacturing Company's mill complex.

The Warren Manufacturing Company from the river.

Employees of the Warren Manufacturing Company shown in the office. Included in this photograph are Annie Lonergan, Henry Champlin, Alfred Barton, and Willard Hoar.

Cutler Mills, which manufactured hosiery yarns, on Cutler Street, 1881.

The Parker Mill on Metacom Avenue, constructed in 1879 when this part of town was still relatively undeveloped.

Parker Mills.

Burr's Tavern. Shubael Burr kept a tavern at the southwest corner of Main and Washington (previously King) Streets before the Revolution. Originally a house, Burr turned it into a tavern by adding an extension to the north. In 1775 he became postmaster and the building served as Warren's post office. Letters waiting to be collected were displayed in a front window. Mrs. Burr was among those harassed by Hessian soldiers during the British raid on Warren in 1778. Burr's Tavern hosted many distinguished guests including George Washington (on March 13, 1781), Thomas Jefferson, the Marquis de Lafayette, and Israel Putnam. In his *Travels in North America*, the Marquis de Castellux recorded "I alighted at a good inn the master of which, called Buhr, is remarkable for his size, as well as that of his wife and all his family." After Burr's death in 1790, the building reverted to a dwelling again. When Burr's Tavern was demolished in the early 1900s, local historian Virginia Baker lamented the loss of Warren's ties with an illustrious past.

Cole's Hotel, famed for its cookery, established by Deacon Ebenezer Cole in 1762. After his death in 1799 at the age of eighty-four, Ebenezer's son, Colonel Benjamin Cole, took over and added a "Hall" where many meetings and social affairs were held. The hotel burned down in 1893.

The construction of Goff's Hotel on the site of Cole's Hotel.

The Commercial Hotel, Market Street.

Goff s Hotel. Jeremiah and Maggie Goff, who were the proprietors of Cole's Hotel at the time of the fire, chose to name their new building Goff's Hotel.

The New Fessenden House, at the corner of Main and Croade Streets. This building, which became a hotel after the Civil War, was originally the home of General Guy M. Fessenden, Warren's first published historian.

HOTEL WARREN, SHOWING TOWER OF TOWN HALL
WARREN, R. I.

The updated Fessenden Hotel, pictured here during the 1930s. The Fessenden Hotel became the Hotel Warren, and was the Warren Manor when it burned down in 1994.

Malloy's Market, on the west side of north Water Street.

Horses and carts outside Fulton's Market, at the junction of north Water Street and Bowen1Street.

W.T. Dunwell's carriage shop on Water Street, located next to Staples Coal Yard close to the foot of State Street.

G.R. Cole's blacksmith shop, located east of the railroad on Market Street.

The Charles E. Clark Meat Market near the corner of Main and Market Streets. Next door is C.M. Wilbur, Undertaking.

The 1906 construction of the Industrial Trust Building, Main Street (the Fleet Bank today), on the site of the National Warren Bank.

The Industrial Trust Company and the telephone buildings.

Miller Street looking west from Main Street in 1890.

Stores on the north side of Miller Street. These stores were later replaced by the Lyric Theater, which has now become the Warren Antiques Center.

Miller Street viewed from Main Street, showing the Lyric Theater in 1947.

The Post Office and Telephone Exchange, on the west side of Main Street, opposite Goff's Hotel. In 1890 the exchange had forty subscribers with one telephone line to Providence, one line to Fall River, one line to Boston, and one line to New York.

Sparks Hardware store on Main Street.

The interior of a Warren shoe store at the turn of the century.

The Main Street Garage and J. Heon's Drug Store, Main Street.

The interior of a dry goods store in Warren.

A. Dio's Dry Goods and Kitchen Ware store on Main Street.

The Ideal 5 & 10 Store.

Three sober-looking individuals outside a bar.

The interior of a store selling meats, groceries, and fruits at 7 Child Street.

Main Street looking south from Church Street showing the commercial district. The town hall was dedicated in 1894. Its tower (in the center) was severely damaged in the 1938 hurricane, necessitating the reduction of its original 125 feet.

Five

Summer Pastimes

A vacation cottage in south Warren, which developed as a summer colony.

The Charles Whipple Greene family, in a photograph labeled "Laura, John, Charlotte Alice, M. Boyde, Frank, Charley, Olin, and May."

The Charles Whipple Greene House, c. 1890, on South Main Street. The family is shown here out on the porch enjoying the summer weather. Charles Whipple Greene, an insurance agent, was active in civic and political organizations in town.

The Van Sickle House, Bridge Street, with striped summer awnings.

Apiary in the side yard (beside the Baptist church) of the DeWolf House on Main Street.

Greene's Landing, at the foot of Beach Street.

Summer cottages at Greene's Landing.

The Gladding family enjoying a summer outing.

Warren Beach around 1900.

A postcard of the lower dam on the Kickemuit River.

Pastoral Warren in 1907.

An ice house on the Kickemuit River.

"On Kickemuit's Zigzag Stream." The meandering course of the river was said to have been caused by a giant eel in a Native American legend.

A postcard showing the Kickemuit Road looking south.

Six

Getting Around Town

A donkey cart at the corner of Main and Child Streets.

Child Street looking east from Main Street. The man crossing the street is using stepping stones.

Main Street looking north east from Baker Street. A tethered horse awaits its rider.

A horse and cart outside G.R. Cole's blacksmith shop.

Cyrus Peabody's hardware store, built in 1876 at the corner of Main and State Streets. The Union Club was housed upstairs, as was the Warren Library and its reading rooms until it moved to the new library in 1889. In front of the store are early bicycles and a delivery wagon.

A bicycle shop in Warren in the 1920s.

Tom Gallagher and Ira Hall on a horse drawn streetcar, in a photograph taken on Main Street at the junction of Church Street.

A trolley heading down Market Street.

A train crossing the railroad bridge, in a view looking toward Barrington.

The railroad station at Warren center.

Warren Station on Railroad Avenue, at the foot of Joyce Street.

Engine 222 at the Warren Station in 1891.

A train crossing the Kickemuit River in August 1897.

Foreman and Carpenter's delivery wagon on Main Street.

A delivery from Staples Coal Yard on Water Street at the foot of State Street.

The horse-drawn delivery wagon of N. Paquin, a Warren grocer.

West side of Main Street, looking north from the town hall. Both horse-drawn vehicles and automobiles lined the streets during this transitional period.

Kelly's Bridge. A toll bridge built in 1802 replaced the ferry that ran to Barrington.

Kelly's Bridge and Tide-Mill, located across Palmer River between Barrington and Warren. This was a favorite spot for fishing in the 1880s.

78

Construction work on the new Kelly's Bridge in 1890, from Barrington.

The most recent Warren Bridge.

A garage in town, *c.* 1920s. Once the age of the automobile arrived, several garages like this one opened in town.

Main Street, looking south.

Seven

Gathering Together

A baseball game, possibly at "The Piggery" on the north side of Franklin Street, between the railroad and present-day Metacom Avenue.

A Warren baseball club, 1908. From left to right are as follows: (front row) unknown, Joseph Foley, unknown, William Smith, William Ryan, and Fred LaFlamme; (middle row) James Parks, James Lonergan, Joseph Wiley, unknown, Charles Kelly, and John Simister Jr.; (back row) John McPike and John Simister Sr. This photograph was taken at "The Piggery," Franklin Street, and shows the wall of South Cemetery and "Child's Woods" in the background.

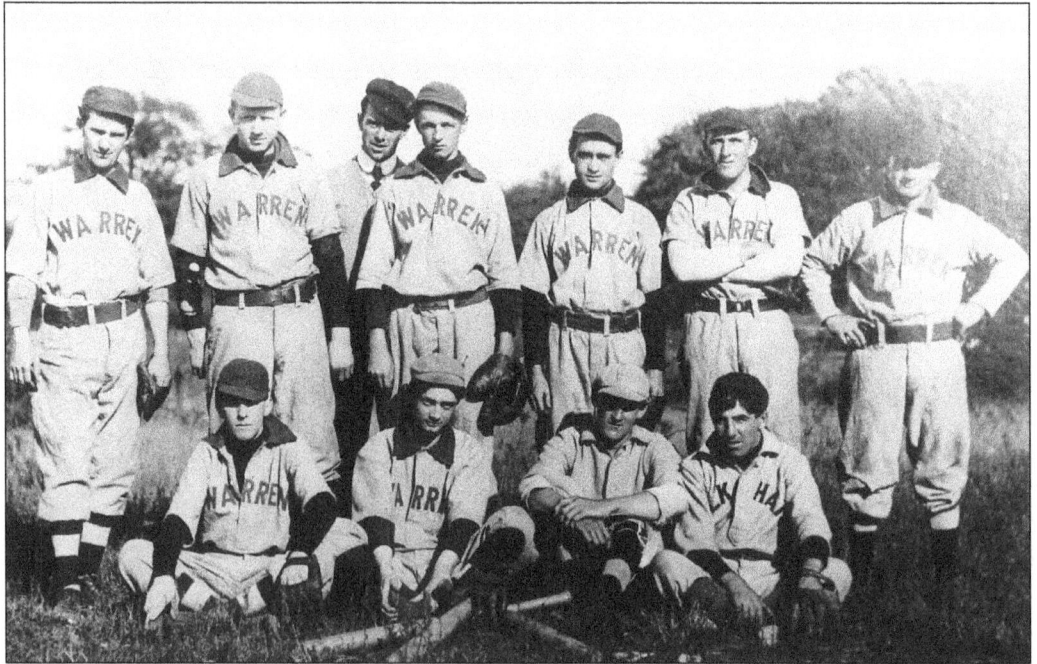

The champions of the Manufacturer's League, 1908–10. From left to right are as follows: (front row) William Ryan, William Smith, Joseph Wiley, and Joseph St. Peter; (back row) Charles Kelley, John Simister, Curtis Chapelle, Howard Martin, Fred LaFlamme, James Lonergan, and James Parkes.

The champions of the Manufacturer's League, 1912. From left to right are as follows: (front row) Edward Conrick, William Beauregard, unknown, Joseph St. Peter, and Herman Heuberger; (middle row) Fred LaFlamme, Walter Beauregard, and Donat Fortier; (back row) Joseph Wiley, Joseph Rockett, Curtis Chapelle, William Ryan, John Simister, Howard Martin, and James Parks.

"The Independents," 1923–24 champions of the Warren Twilight League. From left to right are as follows: (front row) D. Lanoue, Arel, Emmett, B. Riopel, Regnere, and J. Riopel (bat boy); (back row) Gladu, Proulx, Simister, Fitton, and Asselin.

A 1910 Warren baseball club. From left to right are as follows (front row) Herman Heuberger, William Smith, Curtis Chappelle, James Parks, and John Simister; (back row) Joseph St. Peter, Howard Martin, Joseph Wiley, Fred LaFlamme, William Ryan, and James Lonergan.

A c. 1920s Warren baseball team.

The Warren Ladies Seminary. Sometimes known as the Young Ladies Seminary, this school opened on May 7, 1834, with seventy-five pupils and five teachers. Situated on North Main Street between Wood and Hope Streets, it offered young ladies a "systematic, liberal, and thorough" education in a three-year course of instruction. Particular attention was paid to those who wished to become teachers.

An artist's rendition of the Ladies Seminary. By 1857 the school had expanded to 112 students, a principal, and 10 teachers. The curriculum included arithmetic, geometry, algebra, trigonometry, reading, spelling, grammar, composition, rhetoric, history, ancient history, ecclesiastical history, mythology, geography, natural and moral philosophy, natural theology, botany, chemistry, geology, practical astronomy, Latin, Greek, French, drawing, painting, ornamental needlework, and piano. A course of twenty-four lessons in penmanship was offered at no extra charge. Pupils also had "daily opportunities for practice in calisthenics" designed to "produce grace in motion and ease in manners."

During the 1840s, a seminary student, Clara S. Brayton, wrote about Warren: "Warren is a pleasant village situated between Providence and Bristol on a river of the same name. It is bounded north by Rehoboth, east by Swansey, south by Bristol, and west by Barrington. The population is about three thousand. Its inhabitants are generally industrious, steady, and respectable. It contains about a dozen schools among which is the Ladies Seminary where the higher branches of education are taught. Warren is a small seaport place and its inhabitants are engaged in commerce with foreign nations. It contains three churches, the Baptist, Methodist, and Episcopal. It is a pleasant little place although it presents but little variety. It has but one printing office which sends out every Saturday a paper by the name of 'The Northern Star'. Some people like Warren better than others, and as it is my native home, I am inclined to think well of it."

On April 18, 1862, a fire severely damaged the seminary. It was repaired and refurbished only to be completely destroyed by fire less than a year later on April 16, 1863.

The Cambell School, located on a site opposite the present Mechanics Fire Station on Water Street. The "Cambell Schools," two in number, were established for "gratuitous instruction of the children whose parents were unable to pay the tuition." Nicholas Campbell, born in Malta in 1732, came to America before the Revolution, participated in the Boston Tea Party, and served in the Rhode Island Regiment before settling in Warren after the Revolution. Although he could not read or write he left a bequest of approximately $5,000 to be applied to education, administered by a self-perpetuating board of three trustees.

The Miller Street School from the Methodist church spire.

The Miller Street Elementary School, *c.* 1895.

The Joyce Street School, built in 1903. Students were not permitted to walk on the lawns surrounding the building.

The Vernon Street School, c. 1908. The following students have been identified, counting from the far left: (front row) Bernice Dickerson (6th) and Margaret O'Neil (9th); (middle row) Eleanor O'Neil (6th), Edna Bander (11th), and May O'Neil (12th); (back row) John Howland (3rd), Joseph Gillen (4th), twins Clinton and Clayton Mabey (6th and 8th), Alice Rockett (7th), Walton Smith (9th), and Joseph Doherty (10th).

The Liberty Street School, 1847, designed by Thomas Teft. This was the third public high school in Rhode Island. It served as both a high school and a grammar school.

Students at the Liberty Street School, 1886.

The Warren High School Class of 1919. From left to right are as follows: (front row) Eleanor O'Neil Graham, Evelyn Clark, Ada Seymour, Neissen, Beatrice Brown, and Mae O'Neil; (back row) Richmond Staples, Louise Seymour, Mildred Stevens, Ruth Adams, Leo Boutin, Gladys Viall, Ruth Block, Martin McDonough.

Warren High School, built in 1927.

A graduation picture. From left to right are as follows: (front row) Pauline Bloch, Ted Barton, Helen Heuberger, John Conley, Donalda Asselin, unknown, Irene Bullock, Walter Gonzonbach, and Eileen Henley; (second row) Everett Childs, Anna Statchowiak, John Cady, unknown, unknown, Ida Cloutier, Mike McCann, Beatrice Henley, and Bruno Wisnoski; (third row) unknown, Alice Hall, Bob O'Neil, Helena Walsh, Gertrude Gilbert, Percy Gibbs, ? Gifford, and Jim Redfern; (back row) teacher Pauline Kempp, Olive Watjen, Edith Bloch, John Harkins, teacher Mary O'Brien, Bill Myers, Anna Woodley, Anne Higgins, Ethel Warner, teacher Hannah Welch, and ? McCam.

A Warren school photograph: (front row) Hezekiah Butterworth, Florinde Daniels, Ignatius Delekta, and Thomas Byrnes; (second row) Frank Littlefield, Beatrice Sullivan, Anna Kutowski, Howard Turner, Clara Vitullo, Americo Saviano, Dorothy Martin, and Mary Sarao; (third row) Ethel Evers, Francis Spear, Madeline Lavender, Mildred Franklin, James Sarao, Alice Merchant, John Serquoitz, and Madeleine Cady; (back row) Victor Roy, John Smith, Rose Blouin, Eva Gunter, Mary Lebida, and Marguerite Cappuccilli.

92

The George Hail Free Library, Main Street. The library began in 1871 as the Warren Public Reading Room Association and opened on the second floor of a commercial building at the corner of Main and Market Streets. By 1876, when it moved to Cyrus Peabody's building on Main Street, the library had 3,200 volumes. In 1882 Martha Hail, desiring to perpetuate her husband's memory, made a substantial bequest on the condition that the name was changed. This bequest, along with gifts from John Davol and John O. Waterman, provided sufficient funds for the new library building in 1889. From the beginning, the upper floor served as the antiquarian rooms, now the Charles Whipple Greene Museum, a home for a collection of Warren-related materials and artifacts.

The Warren Grange, an organization founded to promote improvements in agriculture. The Grange was formed in 1891 in east Warren, where farming was concentrated. Grange Hall on Child Street was the third home of the organization.

The Masonic Temple, Baker Street. In May 1798, Ebenezer Cole and Sylvester Child were appointed to purchase land for the erection of a building for Washington Lodge #3. Situated on the northeast corner of Baker and Lewin Streets, the temple was completed in the same year. In 1824 the Warren Academy began holding classes on the first floor while the upper story remained for the exclusive use of the lodge. Later, Judge Randall (also the town clerk) used the lower floor for his office and Justice Court Room. It served as the town hall until the present town hall was built on Main Street.

The Masonic Temple, restored in 1914. The lodge room on the upper floor was decorated with mural paintings of Egyptian design by Warren house painter Max Muller.

The Armory on Jefferson Street. Shortly after the Dorr War (1842), the Warren Artillery erected this armory, financed by both town and state funds.

The Warren Artillery, with Charles Whipple Greene in the front center. The Warren Artillery was chartered in 1842 to support Rhode Island's government during the Dorr War, a rebellion centered on the extension of franchise to create a more representative legislature. For their services to the state, the Warren Artillery were given two guns, the "Pallas" and the "Tantae," which had been captured from the British in 1777, during the Revolutionary War.

The Warren Artillery outside the Armory on Jefferson Street.

The Warren Artillery gun squad at "The Piggery" on Franklin Street.

The Warren Artillery with one of its Revolutionary War guns, on Waterman's Wharf.

The Warren Artillery in front of the Armory on Jefferson Street. Those shown in this picture include Alfred Johnson, Howard I. Martin, Mabie (first name not listed), and Frank Maxwell.

The site of Massasoit's Spring, at the foot of Baker Street on the west side of Water Street. The monument consists of a boulder, which was transported from the farm of Hugh Cole (the area's first permanent settler) and donated by one of his descendants, Miss Abby A. Cole; and a tablet, on which is inscribed: "This Tablet placed beside the gushing water known for many generations as Massasoit's Spring commemorates the great Indian Sachem Massasoit, friend of the white man, ruler of this region when the Pilgrims of the Mayflower landed at Plymouth in the year of our Lord 1620."

Massasoit's Spring before the site was purchased and improved. The "true" location of Sowams, Massasoit's home, and the spring that bears his name were lively topics for discussion between Warren historian Virginia Baker and Barrington historian Thomas Bicknell. The "proofs" were set forth and refuted in the two towns' newspapers since civic pride was at stake. In 1806 Jesse Baker and Captain Martin Bowen excavated the spring to a depth of 8 feet and walled it up like a well. A sluice was left for the water to run down to the river. Later a pump covered the site.

Ceremonies on October 19, 1907, at the town hall, after the Massasoit Monument Association unveiled the tablet.

The committee formed to mark Massasoit's Spring and their guests gathered in front of the Joyce Street School for a formal photograph on October 19, 1907. Those shown in the picture include Charles W. Abbot Jr. (president of the Massasoit Monument Association), Charles H. Handy (vice president), Eugene A. Vaughan (secretary), Charles W. Greene (treasurer), as well as Charles W. Cutler, Joseph A. Fauteux, Cornelius Harrington, Joseph Hutcheson, and Frank W. Smith, members of the committee. Warren historian Virginia Baker and Miss Abby A. Cole were among the guests. Alonzo Harris Mitchell and Charlotte Levinia Mitchell, who "bears the Indian name of Wootonekanusk," were present as lineal descendants in the eighth generation from Massasoit.

The Baptist church, 1844, on Main Street. Designed by Russell Warren, this was the third church to be built at this site. The original Brown University, then called Rhode Island College, began here in 1764.

The Methodist church from the Common. The current building was dedicated on October 15, 1845, and replaced an earlier church on the same site on Church Street. In 1848, the Town of Warren placed a clock in the tower.

A stereopticon view dated June 14, 1874. A.G. Eldredge of Warren produced this view, which shows the "Floral Festival—The Sabbath School of the Methodist Episcopal Church, Rev. Dr. Talbot, pastor, held a unique, beautiful, impressive service last evening for the purpose of raising funds to aid indigent young men in seeking an education to fit them for the work of the ministry. An immense audience filled the church, which was beautifully trimmed with flowers, the pulpit and altar rail being fairly changed into a floral garden . . . A rich flower cross stood upon the reading desk of the pulpit with vases on either side . . . The officers, teachers, and scholars of the Sunday school being in the . . . galleries, conducting all the musical portion of the services. Addresses were made . . . recitations by two young ladies were excellently rendered. The singing was superior, and the collection generous."

The rear gallery of the Methodist church from a stereopticon view taken on June 15, 1874. The organ, built by Simmons of Boston, was installed in 1855 at a cost of $2,000.

The Methodist parsonage, west of the church.

St. Mark's Episcopal Church, 1829, on Linden Street, designed by Russell Warren. The square tower was removed after the 1954 hurricane.

St. Mary's Catholic Church. The first church of St. Mary of the Bay, built in 1851, was destroyed by fire on November 6, 1885. This church, built at the corner of Main and Luther Streets, replaced it.

The Narragansett Fire Company with their engine, the "Little Hero," at an event in Providence. The "Little Hero," purchased in 1802 and now proudly displayed in Warren's fire museum, was a hand tub supplied with water by a bucket brigade.

The Mechanics Fire Company No. 2, North Water Street, 1881.

The Mechanics Fire Company No.2 in front of the fire station doors.

The Mechanics Fire Company's fife and drum band.

An informal photograph of the Mechanics Fire Company taken in 1927.

The Rough and Ready Fire Company No. 5 on Metacom Avenue around 1900.

The Rough and Ready Fire Company.

The state champion running team of the Rough and Ready Fire Company. From left to right are unknown, Samuel Boeniger, Henry Turner, Joseph St. Peter, unknown, and Joshua Turner (foreman).

Eight

At the Mercy of the Elements

The aftermath of the October 3, 1895 fire. The Warren Manufacturing Company owned three mills which were destroyed in the "Great Fire of October 3rd, 1895," which burned for days. While the embers of the blaze were still hot, people were moving out of town to seek employment elsewhere.

The stark silhouette of the mill chimney after the October 3, 1895 fire.

A view of the fire-ravaged mill from the water.

The Miller Street School on the corner of Miller and Lewin Streets, after the fire in 1941, seen from Lewin Street looking north. Dedicated in 1871, this school was two stories high and had four classrooms. The boys' entrance was on the south side, the girls' on the north. During the Depression, the upstairs rooms were used to cook and serve meals to the needy. The American Legion had their headquarters in this building for many years. The Narragansett Fire Company built their building on the site.

Cole's Hotel after the disastrous fire on March 25, 1893, which destroyed the building.

Greene's Oyster House at the end of Beach Street, iced in, during severe winter weather.

The Captain James W. Barton House, 37 Liberty Street, c. 1850, after a snowstorm.

A snowy Main Street, looking north from the town hall.

A winter scene of Goff s Hotel (on the north side of Main Street) and a "Ladies and Gents Eating Saloon" that offers "oysters in all styles" and "Boston baked beans."

St Mark's Episcopal Church after the 1938 hurricane.

Trees downed by the hurricane on Washington Street.

The oyster boat G.H. *Church* blocking the roadway, swept there by the force of the 1938 hurricane.

A hurricane-damaged boat at the Warren bridge.

A shipwreck on Warren Beach, *c.* 1900.

Nine

Civic Celebrations

The 1890 Fourth of July Parade down Main Street. On the left is a reviewing stand in front of the Baptist church. In the center is the "new brick store opposite the Baptist Meeting House" where in 1809 Pascal Allen advertised "a general assortment of fall and winter goods selected from the latest importations of ships *Galen* and *Ceres* from London and Liverpool." On the right is the National Warren Bank (predecessor of the Industrial Trust Bank building), a local landmark known for its striking "peach-bloom" color.

Parade Day, Main Street, looking south from State Street.

The Oddfellows Hall on Main Street, decorated for a parade day.

The Tavares Building on Main Street decked with parade bunting.

A "Horribles" parade, a long tradition in Warren.

The Pageant of Warren, October 9, 10, and 12, 1914. This pageant was given by "the people of Warren, assisted by the people of Swansea, Barrington, and Bristol" in honor of the 150th anniversary of the founding of the First Baptist Church of Warren, at Maxwellton, the estate of James Maxwell Wheaton, Esquire. It consisted of a series of tableaux portraying Warren's history accompanied by narration, dancing, and music. Shown here are the Maids O'Mist, representing the mist driven out by the south wind: "the Mists move forward and backward to slow music . . . the South Wind comes dancing driving the Mists before her . . . crosses the brook to the cornfield where the Indian women enter."

Meeting of the Chiefs. "Massasoit and the Pokanoket Indians subject themselves to Canonicus, great sachem of the Narragansetts." Local townspeople portray Native Americans who played a role in Warren's history, including Massasoit (Dr. N.R. Hall), Anawan (Max Muller), "King Philip" (C.C. Bliss), and Canonicus (D.M. Morrisey).

Minute Men. "The part sustained by Warren in the Revolutionary War was an honorable one. At the breaking out of hostilities a company of 'Alarm Men' was formed, and later an artillery company."

The Hessian Drummer. "A party of ladies observed a diminutive drummer encumbered with a very large drum, and much the worse for copious draughts of Jamaican rum . . . 'Aunt Nelly West" seized a brass candlestick exclaiming 'We can capture that man!' rushed into the street . . . [and] pointing her weapon at the drummer she commanded him to halt. Pale with terror, the little man staggered back, stammering piteously, 'Don't fire dear ladies, I surrender.' His fair captors surrounded him and triumphantly conducted him into the house, where they locked him securely in a closet."

King George's Troops. The tableau depicts May 25, 1778, when "a party of British and Hessian soldiers under command of Lieutenant Colonel Campbell invaded Warren."

Ten

Characters and Curiosities

Bob Kinicutt, one of Warren's famous "characters," at the railroad station. Often involved in political debates, he was once told (in reference to his short stature), "Bob, I could pick you up and put you in my pocket," to which he replied "If you did you'd have more brains in your pocket than in your head."

The Turner twins, Maxwell Mason Turner and Goodwin Wheaton Turner, born on March 10, 1907. The twins are shown here being wheeled around town in their double wicker baby carriage.

Town resident Phillip Munroe in his stovepipe hat, in front of the Munroe House at the corner of Child and Adams Streets. The house is no longer standing.

A conference on the Cole's Hotel corner, Joyce and Main Streets.

Phillip Munroe.

Miss Virginia Baker (1859–1927), Warren native, historian, author, and schoolteacher. Miss Baker taught at the Cambell School, the Windmill Hill School, and the Miller Street School, later becoming its principal. She published histories of Warren and wrote articles for the *Atlantic Monthly*, *Harper's Magazine*, and *Scribner's Magazine*, along with historical articles for the *Warren Gazette*. She also financed the publication of *Warren in the War of the Revolution*, obtaining a personal bank loan to do so. When sales did not meet expectations, the bank accepted the unsold copies of the book rather than call in the loan.

A collection of Warren dogs in front of Oddfellows Hall, now Delekta's Pharmacy.

"Holding Down the Law in Warren, R.I."

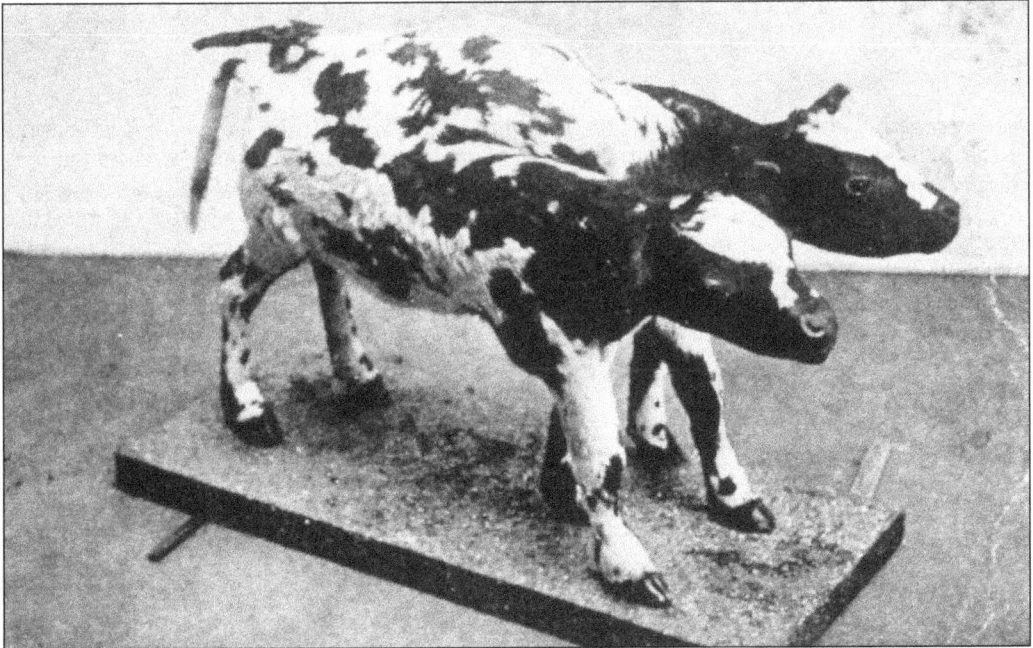
The two-headed calf, delivered, owned, and exhibited by Dr. Conklin.

The South Cemetery Gates, Franklin Street.

Acknowledgments

Putting together this volume would have been impossible without the generosity and support of the Massasoit Historical Association. Most of the photographs come from their Laurent Dionne Memorial Collection, and we appreciate Laurent Dionne's foresight and dedication in assembling it. We thank all those who contributed photographs to it. The George Hail Free Library has also been most generous in lending us a number of photographs from their collection. The Henry Cady photographs were lent by Roland and Joan Rogers and we thank them for this important contribution.

Information for the captions came from several sources, including *The History of Warren, Rhode Island in the War of the Revolution* (1901), by Virginia Baker; *Program and Book of Words of The Pageant of Warren* (1914) by Margaret MacLaren Eager; *200th Anniversary of Warren, Rhode Island: Historical Sketch and Program* (1947) by Henry J. Peck; *Statewide Preservation Report, Rhode Island Historical Preservation Commission: Warren, Rhode Island* (1975) by Elizabeth S. Warren; and *A History of Warren* (unpublished typescript, no date) compiled by Lydia Rogers.

Lastly we would like to thank all the people in Warren who have answered our questions, identified people in photographs, and shared their memories with us. While this is not a complete history of Warren, it is accurate to the best of our knowledge and attempts to present glimpses of Warren's rich and varied heritage.

www.ingramcontent.com/pod-product-compliance
Lightning Source LLC
Chambersburg PA
CBHW080911100426
42812CB00007B/2236